Words of Twenty

Sheliza Nanji

Words of Twenty © 2024 Sheliza Nanji

All rights reserved.

Sheliza Nanji asserts the moral right to be identified as author of this work.

Presentation by *BookLeaf Publishing*

Web: www.bookleafpub.com

E-mail: info@bookleafpub.com

ISBN: 9789358319668

First edition 2024

ACKNOWLEDGEMENT

Thank you to my loved ones for the confidence to be who I am. Thank you to my mentors for the passion to do what I love.

PREFACE

These poems are a mixture of my past and present with hints of the future. I hope you resonate with them in some way, I hope you find comfort and know you aren't alone.

The cap, the gown, and the scroll

They've finally got to the 200s,
The names being called by a professor
Who I have only ever seen,
Yet he pronounces each letter of our names,

Trying desperately to be correct.
I walk up to her and she fixes my sash,
Pulling the grey onto shoulders,
And after adjusts my cap.

The lose thread hangs to the left of my face,
With a historic symbolism I don't really know,
But I know it's important that it's there.

The cap, the gown and the scroll.

And the professor announces my accolades,
Then says my name slowly,
So I smile and walk towards a man who never knew me,
As he hands me a scroll with meaningless words.

But he asks, what did I do for those awards,

And I summarise in two words.

Are two words enough to describe what I did?
The relationships I made along the way?
The 4 years beyond the degree
Which I dedicated my time to each day?

No, two words don't even begin to describe,
But I laugh and smile and walk down the stairs
anyway,
And look at almost everyone I ever loved with
the same grin on their faces.

And I understand,
That those smiles know what I meant,
Those eyes understand the last 4 years of my
life,
Those faces know the effort and struggle that
made me, me.

So it's okay if that man knows two words,
Those who know, know what I mean.
Those who saw, saw within me.
That the cap, the gown and the scroll mean less,

Much less than the hugs I received.

- graduation day
- surrounded by the people who love me

The best of me

I see her in moments,
The same dimpled smile,
The same big laugh.
I know she's rehearsed this,
But it's never what she knows,
Some kind of improv act,
Although I don't think so.
There's a light in the brown,
Of her eyes that grin too.
And a shine like that can't be faked,
Or lied through.
Yet she tries to practise the words to say,
And it's never what she ends up speaking.
Somehow it's better,
Somehow there's more power,
In the rhythm of her voice,
From an honesty I can't explain.
I guess I envy her,
The effortless vulnerability,
Where she finds her power.
But I know I don't need to be,
Because she is who I am,
She is the best of me.
I see her in moments,
Because she is who I am.

And I'm proud of us.

- you are every version of you
- there is no separation

Those trees in Enfield

In -1 degrees,
It stands by the greenery.
With crispy, frozen branches,
And lights that say to me.
"There's brightness where you can't see,
And happiness around these leaves."
So when I find him staring at me,
Telling me we can make the most of this,
I believe everything he says.
And we kiss under the Enfield trees,
Like it was never really -1 degrees.

- a date
- an adventure

Happy pride always

Colours filled the space in every direction you
look at,
Balloons and glitter and flags and signs of
support,
An outward affection, an explicit admiration,
Saying yes, you're here and you're loved no
matter what.
There's a challenge that the existence of joy
should not be here,
That some books are to determine whether you
matter,
And yet you are here, dancing to the beating
hearts of those watching you,
Loving you, and celebrating you.
You are seen by those who fought and are now
resting peacefully, knowing you're being exactly
who you were meant to be.
And I wonder if you've seen the diversity of the
crowd, the people who look like you and me,
The people that showed up so you and I could
feel free.
I know we deserve to feel like this all year
around,
And in a world where hatred is capitalised on,
freedom is a far-fetched thought.

Yet, I still want you know that pride is all year round,
In every moment you feel happy, euphoric and loved, because pride is love and joy,
And queer joy is resistance and love will always prevail.

- pride lasts beyond a month
- pride is forever

Saviour

Every old tale speaks of saviours,
Valiant warriors and courageous hearts,
That ride in on their steeds,
To save a person, a place or the world.

The tales of saviours,
The hope that they will rise,
To fight against any evil or horror,
They'll fix everything.

And when I see humanity,
The remnants of such a tale embodies us,
An individual pushed into being a saviour,
An individual needing to be saved.

The reality of such a tale is grim,
There's more darkness hidden in life,
Not a big heroic moment for the saviour to win,
Because sometimes they don't win.

And sometimes people refuse to be saved,
And sometimes people don't want to save,
And sometimes people don't know how to save,
Or even be saved.

Yet I think we are still inspired enough,
By the tales of saviours to think,
That maybe we are the saviour,
Not of the world but of ourselves.

That saviours don't rise in just a person,
But an army of humanity that simply try,
Try to love and understand others,
To hold someone's hand while they battle.

Maybe the light to shine on hidden darkness,
And the magic of mythical saviours,
Is a smile from a stranger or a phonecall with a
friend,
Or the small "love you" said everytime a
phonecall ends.

- saving ourselves
- by loving
- treat people with kindness

The bittersweet

The bittersweet days exist,
In the measure of two weeks,
Where I've felt moments of happiness,
But an overall weird contentment,
Because its more bittersweet than I've felt.

I've spent the days making memories,
The drawing of permanent marks on my skin,
The photos we take of where we've been,
The hugs with people I met way too recently.

Those moments of happiness I'll remember,
The memories that last till my grave,
Yet I never thought I'd be here.
A day past 18 seemed way too far away.

But here I am on a cold, metal bench,
The nothingness of a blue sky above me,
I wonder if I've done enough, lived enough,
If I've made an impact on the world around me.

And I remember that I'm 5 years past 18,
With an experience detailed through words and
photos,
Of a story I once dreamed of.

The bittersweet days exist,
In the measure of a lifetime,
Yet the moments of my happiness matter more
than I can comprehend.
Here's to a weird contentment,
And this chapter's end.

- weird
- but content
- the end of final year
- the end of uni

For her

The separation occurred,
A long time ago,
Through anger and pain and sorrow,
And I wonder if they knew
That they had halved a person,
Things would have changed.
Yet I don't think so,
Nothing would have stopped,
The rip between us.
Written in the stars was a misalignment,
To carry us to the grave.

I refuse to let this happen,
I refuse to let them win.
I refuse to lose you any further
Before our life would even begin.
So I promise I'll come back to you.
I imagine in front of the sea,
You and I will live life together again,
We will be one within me.

- coming back to myself
- i promise we will be one again
- i owe it to myself to be true to who i am

Winter's air

It's the first time this season,
I've felt calm in winter's air.
The same rush of cars through traffic,
Same buildings everywhere.

Winter's air holds someone's anger,
It holds someone's fear,
But now it holds my peacefulness,
And a ring of festive cheer.

With bare trees surrounding our house,
Where the morning frost is sat,
On the grass crunching with my step,
Winter is where stories are at.

So happy Winter to you sitting in your blanket,
With your fluffy socks and hot tea.
Winter's air may bring its chill,
But I hope the togetherness is what you see.

- winter
- festivity
- calm
- warmth

"Jet Black Heart"

His voice singing the first note
Intranced me straight away
To a bridge I once stood on
On a cold autumn day.
And as he sings the words tonight,
I wonder how much time has gone by,
From the moment of repeatedly playing their
lyrics,
To watching them live as I cry.
And yes I do cry,
As the second verse chimes in,
Because I'd like to think,
The 16 year old healing will begin.
But her healing began a long time ago,
My healing commenced at sixteen,
When this same song played and reminded me,
About what resilience would mean.
Yet the universe knew I needed it now,
For the sound to be screamed in front of me,
To finally let go of the cars running beneath me,
And embrace being free.
It won't be as easy,
The haunting memory ricochets in my darkness,
But for now, in the bright light of the stage,
I am me, healed, healing, happy.

- 5sos London show
- thank you

I choose love

I've been intrigued with the thought that we
choose to love.
Love can embody our very being if we choose to
let it in.
That one day we decide in a moment that yes, I
will choose to love.
I will give love.
I will change the dynamic of the world one step
at a time by loving all of what is around me.
And it is hard to choose love.
When the world in it's state is fighting against
that notion.
That choosing love will not change a thing.
Sometimes it doesn't.
And when we feel like we can't choose love, the
universe will find love for us.

Love in the orange and yellow sunrise every
morning, love in the cup of tea that is brewing,
love in the sight of our messy hair in the mirror,
love in the people that smile while walking, love
in the cafe worker that makes me a hot
chocolate, love in the daily 'how are you' texts,
love in the hot lunch served in the restaurant,
love in the music blasting in our ears on the bus,

love in the new poetry book we're reading, love
in the stars accompanying us on our walk home,
love in loved ones asking 'how was your day',
love in the small wins, love in opening my eyes
the next day.

So I'll choose to love life as it is, and life as it
may become.
Life, 6 years later.

- 6 years clean

The untitled existence of the sea

I cannot see all of you,
And yet I know you're there.
As you come in with every crash,
I'm reminded of the reality of your existence.
You may be vast and unknown,
Something which calls all anxiety.

But what I realise is for the first time, I'm not
scared of the unknown if it's you I'm facing.
With each ebb and flow, my anxiousness fades
away.

Maybe this is what trust is like. The not knowing
but still feeling okay.

- poem 2 of 2 while facing the night time
Mediterranean sea.

Representation matters

It was like I was English outside the house,
And Indian inside.
Rooted in the earth of India,
And somehow bloomed British.
It meant to hide away those Bollywood movies,
And the obsession with Hrithik Roshan,
In the Krrish series.
The British-ness existed explicitly,
I can probably quote you Ben Mitchell's life
story,
While listening to One Direction's Best Song
Ever.

Yet an entire part of me was locked away,
The songs, the dresses, the food was never
displayed,
I even tried to hide my own name,
Most people stopped trying to pronounce it
correctly anyway.
There wasn't anyone to unlock that,
Other than myself when I grew up.
It took years to fall in love with my mixed
culture,
Because kids are mean, mimicking their parents.
But I became proud of my coloured armour,

Rooted in earth, the foundation of my being.

So if I cry over Simone Ashley in Bridgerton,
If I cry over 2 Indian women leading a Western
programme,
If I cry over the Kabhi Khushi Kabhi Gham
instrumental on the show,
If I cry because I see myself in Kate and my
partner in Anthony,
Let me be.

My inner child is healing.

- representation matters
- crying over the soundtrack
- proud to be Indian always

Amaryllis

Each mirror covered with a sheet,
Curtains pulled over, shut doors and windows,
The lights off,
No potential of sunshine pushing through,
No voice reaching in, no reflection seen.
Less of any sparkle, no glint in sight of the
outside finding it's way in.

What's a sparkle?
What's it like to sparkle through the night?
What's it like to not differ to stars, bringing
breakthroughs to disrupt the darkness?
To sparkle is to be fought for,
It's pride. Pride felt when one is completely and
utterly themselves.
Or when one just is. When one exists.
Can one sparkle when they simply live or take a
breath?
And they can. There's pride in just breathing.
Pride in living through darkness when it
surrounds each element of sense.

It's forgotten that light pushes through the
darkest of places.

The glint off the mirror reminding that you are
still there, you are indeed alive and well.
A shred of sun finds its way through closed
curtains, sparkling through each break and bend.
You sparkle.
I think it's magical that the universe wants to
remind you of such.

- from Navroz
- new beginning
- from Spring
- inspired by my tattoo

Finally

"People don't understand because they haven't
been through the hell you've been through."

I think it's commendable,
To walk away from people,
That you have always known.
The same people that know you,
The same people you so easily call close,
The same people that saw only your faults.

I find it commendable,
That you left what was so familiar,
For the complete unknown,
Because you finally said no,
That's enough now,
I've had enough.

I figured we stay in places
That we always have been,
Because its easier to know what we know.
But I'll tell you,
The best decisions were those,
That pushed me to say no.

So I commend you and I,

For finally letting go,
Of something that was always toxic,
But we'd overlook that more and more.
We're better off as we are,
Opening ourselves to what may come.

- letting go
- heaviness
- we deserve better

Building narratives

And I know I've been creating stories ever since
I learnt what it meant to think
The wild imagination was always there
They encouraged it, teachers, they said its
important
And maybe it is but I lived in that wild
imagination
More than I lived in reality
To fantasise and obsess over things that were
never true
Where I could create stories on demand
A talent or a threat to my internal self
A danger to never understand reality because I
was never there
No the danger was building narratives upset
The stories created with intrusive thoughts
Where the talent escaped me
Where it was admirable to not feel, thus to not
think
But that never worked
Because false narratives still build and stay with
you
With every anxiety, every bad moment
Till destruction

To start living was something I learnt when I left
the places I never lived in
But recognising life was still worlds away
And years later I fight the same false narratives
The fakes, the unreal, the battle is still there
Rarer than before
And maybe that's my win
To build narratives only when creative writing
and storytelling and designing and making and
painting
Still fighting but I don't want it to destroy me
And it won't as long as I'm choosing

- imagination
- i was always a storyteller

An apology to my body

Dear you,

I find that writing is what comes easier to me,
though this letter may never be easy, yet
important, important to write and important to
recite, because this is my apology to you.

You with all your crevices and curves, you with
the extra bends of skin, you as you are, ever so
extraordinary.

I'm sorry. I'm sorry to have never appreciated
you in all the glory that you hold. That you
always held. You endured, and you've cried, and
you broke into pieces but you are still here,
keeping each piece of us together. You've had to
do that alone because I always wished to never
be in you.

I'm sorry for causing you such pain. Some of
those scars are from me, from the darkness that
filled me and you had to take a pain that was
never yours.

You were always beautiful. You are beautiful, you are elegant, you are a masterpiece of creation with each scar, each stretch, each bend.

You held me when I scarred you and threw you against the storms. You took each breath persistently despite me trying to stop you, because you knew, you knew I didn't want you to stop.

You wake up each day and you let me see the sun, you let me feel each breeze as if it were only meant for me. And you are meant for me.

You give me the ability to write and paint. You let me tell my stories the way I'd like them to be told.

You took me on the greatest expedition of my life. You, step by step, led me to the sunsets and the starry nights, with only fields to see and nature to submerge in. You encourage me to be with nature, you thrive there.

You let me love, you let me receive such love and make my heart happy when we're hugged.

You were always extraordinary. You are extraordinary.

I'm sorry it's taken me so long to tell you that.

Yours faithfully,

Me

- they say the first step to healing is to apologise
to your body

Ten princesses they said I was

They told me I was the first princess, but I had a
cheeseburger instead of an apple.
So, I became the second princess, but I wore
trainers instead of glass heels.
Princess three slept a lot so maybe I was already
a princess.
Though, the fourth princess had to be kissed so
they censored it on TV.
Princess five read books so I secretly liked her.

Princess six actually looked like me, but she was
one out of fourteen.
My stomach had butterflies when I saw princess
seven, yet girls couldn't marry princesses.
So I sidestepped princess eight, and stayed away
from princess nine,
But I became princess ten,

Because queer brown girls can be princesses too.
Marching hand in hand, raising our bangles,
And tucking our sari ends into our skirts.
We secure our pride flags,
Waving from the castle they told us we couldn't
have.

- i'm a princess as i am
- so are you

What I should have said

That you're not even trying to say it correctly
That you'd like me to shorten it for you

"It's pronounced Sha-lee-za, actually."

That you can erase my identity in a single
moment
That you assume I'm not British

"It's pronounced Sha-lee-za, actually."

That you see it in the register and get scared of
saying it
That you deny me the job because my name's
too 'Indian-sounding'

"It's pronounced Sha-lee-za, actually."

That you can say Schwarzenegger
That you can say Tchaikovsky

"It's pronounced Sha-lee-za, actually."

That you think I'm rude when I correct you
That you think it's "too hard"

"It's pronounced Sha-lee-za, actually."

That you know I'll be waiting to correct it
That you know I'm used to it but you don't care

"It's pronounced Sha-lee-za, actually."

- you can say my name
- you don't care enough to learn how
- i wish i corrected you

"She looks like,"

I can't tell you
What to feel
When you see
Me, how I look
Is mostly
What comes to your mind
Nothing else
Attraction
Is she attractive
To be judged on a look
Judged on a face
Fixed with imperfections
We're human, for God's sake
And if I start
Telling you
How I think you look
You'll feel the same
But I won't
Because I'm not you
I'm not just anyone
She looks like a man
You said to them
Laughing
Continuing
She's not attractive

You say to them
And I confess
Back then I didn't
Think I was attractive
Good looking was far off
Pretty was even further
But now I have courage
To call you out
On your stupid ideologies
Of how I should look
And society has brainwashed you
So you think I should look like them
Well surprise
I'm not them
Why would I look like them
I like me
I look good
I look great according to myself
And this confidence has come
Just recently
Back then I would have cried
I would have not taken any pictures
Of me
Of my face
Of my arms
Of my legs
But now
I know me
I am me

I have the confidence
So you can rot away
I'm not like all those fruit flies
Why should I chase you
When I have everything I need
Right inside me
So yes she looks like a man
To you
And that's fine
Because she looks like her
To me
And that's what is most
Important

- from a few years ago
- a comment from a little man
- i love me as i am

Moments of metamorphosis

Moments of metamorphosis,
The thought consumes me.
Awaiting those life-changing seconds,
That cause most to thrill seek.
And I don't doubt,
That moments of magic
Connect with each thrill and ride,
It brings me joy to see that.
Yet I wait for the moment,
This big defining moment,
That will give me some sort of purpose,
Where my perspective will transform.
Although lately, I've been learning,
That moments of metamorphosis,
Already exist around me,
And I've felt them.

The cap, the gown and scroll I received,
Giving a winning speech in April,
The offer of a job role,
The selection as a leader.
Three months of amazing volunteering,
The results of my exams,
The results of my degree,
The placement offer I had.

When my mom and I dressed in saris,
The new book I started reading.
The calming tones of therapeutic hope,
And future talks with Alex.
When I bought my Dad an oodie with dogs,
When Chinmay taught me skincare.
My brother bought me chicken wings.
And when I finished the Avatar novel.
When I visited my best friends in Brighton,
And Sheetal painted a shark.
When I followed Lizzie around the Artbox cafe,
And we sat and ate and laughed.

Moments of metamorphosis exist,
In the seconds of small joys.
When in reality those joys are biggest moments,
Moments of confidence, love and change.

- embrace the little things
- they help you grow, as well as the big things

Fight until they are free

Liberation is for all,
Or none of us are free.
The days in which the modern world,
Is witnessing a war, digitally.
And we follow heroes,
Human like you and me,
Except in press vests,
Holding little cats,
And guarding olive trees.
Yet I wonder if you remember,
Heroes are not what they wanted to be.
Humans like you and me,
They wanted to live freely.
Taking pictures, having sugar and playing by the
sea.
So I ask you to keep fighting,
As digital soldiers sharing and donating,
As global protestors marching and yelling,
As boaters kayaking in front of a large ship,
As journalists constantly updating the world,
As commuters with watermelon keyrings on
their bags.
Keep fighting until they are free.

- Free Palestine, Free Sudan, Free Congo, Free
Tigray, Free all of those that need to be freed
- no one is free until they are free
- what you do now is what you would have done
during the wars, during slavery, this will be on
your conscience
- no amount of words are enough
- donate:
https://www.islamic-relief.org.uk/giving/appeals
/palestine/
https://donate.unrwa.org/gaza
https://donate.palestinecampaign.org/
https://humanappeal.org.uk/appeals/sudan-emerg
ency-appeal
https://www.oxfam.org.uk/oxfam-in-action/curre
nt-emergencies/democratic-republic-congo/
https://www.worldvision.org.uk/emergencies/tigr
ay-crisis-appeal/